The month of March, from the illuminated manuscript *Les Trés Riches Heures du duc de Berry*

The Story of a Special Day
Volume 89

March

29

88th day of the year
(89th in leap years)
277 days remaining
until the end of the year.

by Michael Dobson

Timespinner
Press

Table of Contents

Cover: Soldiers from China's Terracotta Army — for the Event of the Day.

Pearl Bailey

March 29 Quotations

"Typical Hollywood crowd — all the kids are on drugs and all the adults are on roller skates."

— Eric Idle, British comedian, member of Monty Python, born March 29, 1943

"What the world really needs is more love and less paper work."

— Pearl Bailey, singer and actress, born March 29, 1918

"The only thing that saves us from the bureaucracy is inefficiency. An efficient bureaucracy is the greatest threat to liberty."

— Eugene McCarthy, US Senator and presidential candidate, born March 29, 1916

"You bring me the man, I'll find you the crime."

— Lavrentiy Beria (Лаврéнтий Бéрия), chief of the Soviet secret police under Stalin, born March 29, 1899

"The first $100,000 — that was hard to get; but afterwards it was easy to make more."

— John Jacob Astor, first US millionaire, died March 29, 1848

"A life of kindness is the primary meaning of divine worship."

— Emanuel Swedenborg, engineer and philosopher, founder of Swedenborgianism, died March 29, 1772

Excavation of part of the Teracotta Army.
A large arched hall was built over the original site.

Event of the Day
Discovery of the Terracotta Army

On March 29, 1974, three farmers were digging a well east of the Chinese city of Xi'an when they discovered ancient terracotta pottery shards not too far from the Mausoleum of the First Qin Emperor. When a team of Chinese archeologists came to investigate, what they found was far beyond anyone's imagining — an army consisting of over 8,000 life-sized terracotta figures, along with 130 chariots pulled by 520 horses and another 150 calvary horses, along with Chinese court officials and entertainers.

This was part of the amazing funeral complex for the first emperor of a unified China, Qin Shi Huang (born 259 BCE, died 210 BCE). Born Zhao Zheng (although it is taboo to say his given name), Wang (King) of the feudal state of Qin, the future emperor conquered the various independent states that made up modern China, ending the Warring States period of Chinese history. He unified China around 221 BCE, and work on his mausoleum began within a few years.

Records of the time are prone to the exaggeration that was an all too common element of early history. According to an account written by Sima Qian about a hundred years after the Qin Emperor's death, over 700,000 laborers worked to build his necropolis (city of the dead)— unlikely, because not even the largest cities in the world at that time had as many as 700,000 residents. A more recent calculation suggests that a mere 16,000 men could have built the foundations in only two years, and the entire complex took forty years to build.

The Terracotta Army itself was made on an assembly line basis. Heads, arms, legs, and torsos were created in different workshops. Eight basic face molds created the likenesses, after which clay was added to make each face truly individual. As the pieces arrived, they were assembled and placed in the pits in military formations. The weapons they held were made of metal, and many have inscriptions that suggest they had been used in actual battle. The figures were originally painted, but the colors have either flaked off or faded with the passage of time.

The figures are located in four main pits: the first contains the main army; the second is filled with cavalry and chariots; the third is a command post with high-ranking officers. The fourth is empty, evidently left unfinished. The pits were originally roofed over before the accumulation of centuries buried the site altogether.

The Terracotta Army was there to guard the Qin Emperor's actual mausoleum, which has not yet been excavated because of its antiquity and the care needed not to damage the priceless artifacts. It's buried under a 76-meter (250-foot) mound disguised as a normal hill, with trees and vegetation planted on top. In addition to the Terracotta Army standing guard, the mausoleum is surrounded by a replica of the Emperor's capital city, Xianyang. The inner city is 2.5 km (about a mile and a half) in circumference and the outer city stretches to 6.3 km (nearly four miles).

Because the tomb has not been excavated, we must rely on current accounts for our knowledge. Sima Quian wrote, "Palaces and scenic towers for a hundred officials were constructed, and the tomb was filled with rare artifacts and wonderful treasure. ... Mercury was used to simulate ... the Yangtze and Yellow River ... and set to flow mechanically. Above were representations of the heavenly constellations, below, the features of the land." Modern technology has been able to detect some of the features of the walled city and a massive palace nearly a quarter of the size of Beijing's Forbidden City. As far as the mercury rivers are concerned, high levels of mercury have been found in the area of the tomb mound.

As was common, the Emperor's concubines were ordered to "accompany the dead" into the tomb. While the ordinary laborers were set free, the specialized craftsmen who built the mechanical devices for the tomb complex were left inside the tomb at the end of the funeral ceremonies, and died there.

The majority of the Terracotta Army are still in their original formations, but some have travelled. An exhibition of 20 warriors and 120 artifacts from the mausoleum was the most popular show at the British Museum in London as well as in the Forum de Barcelona. The exhibition has travelled to Chile, Sweden, San Francisco, Houston, Atlanta, Washington, and Toronto.

The Terracotta Army and the Mausoleum of the Qin Emperor have been named a UNESCO World Heritage Site, reserved for places considered to have outstanding universal value as part of the world's cultural and natural heritage. Fewer than one thousand sites worldwide carry that distinction.

National Lemon Chiffon Cake Day (Photo: Kimberly Vardeman)

March 29 Holidays and Celebrations

Boganda Day (Central African Republic)

Boganda Day commemorates the death of Barthélemy Boganda (April 4, 1910 to March 29, 1959). Boganda negotiated the independence of the Central African Republic from France in 1958. He served as the first prime minister during the transition from autonomous territory to state, and was planning to serve as his country's first president following independence when he died in a mysterious plane crash. Experts found traces of explosives in the wreckage, but the perpetrators are unknown — though there are many suspects.

Boganda Day, celebrated on March 29 each year, is a public holiday in the Central African Republic.

Día del Joven Combatiente (Chile)

The Day of the Young Combatant in Chile each March 29 commemorates the deaths of the brothers Rafael and Eduardo Vergara Toledo during the military regime era in that country. It is marked by violence directed at the Chilean government, including throwing rocks and Molotov cocktails.

Martyrs' Day (Madagascar)

The people of Madagascar rebelled unsuccessfully against French colonial rule beginning on March 29, 1947, in what is known as the Malagasy Uprising. A brutal French military response put down the rebellion, with a death toll estimated by various sources as somewhere between

11,000 and 90,000, with the French government acknowledging that the French military had committed war crimes in putting down the rebels.

March 29 is commemmorated in Madagascar as Martyr's Day. The nation of Madagascar finally achieved independence, becoming an autonomous state in 1958 and full independence in 1960.

National Lemon Chiffon Cake Day (United States)

In the United States, almost every day of the year is dedicated to a particular food. Sponsored by manufacturers, retailers, farmers, or simply fans, these days are often proclaimed by the President, Congress, state governors, or mayors.

March 29 is National Lemon Chiffon Cake Day. Chiffon cakes are a combination of batter and foam style cakes, made fluffy by the addition of beaten egg whites, and are so moist they tend not to dry out. They don't, however, have the same rich flavor as cakes made with butter, so they usually are served with an assortment of fillings or sauces. Chiffon cake was invented in 1927 by California caterer (and former insurance salesman) Harry Baker. He kept the recipe a secret for twenty years, then sold it to General Mills, who published fourteen chiffon cake recipes in a 1946 Betty Crocker pamphlet. Of the many sorts of chiffon cake, lemon chiffon is one of the most popular.

Youth Day (Republic of China/Taiwan)

Many nations around the world declare special days to celebrate the youth of their countries. In the Republic of China (Taiwan), it is celebrated on March 29 to commemorate the Yellow Flower Mound Revolt (Second Guangzhou Uprising) of 1911, in which 72 young people died trying to overthrow the Qing Dynasty.

Christian Feast Days

In *Western Christianity*, saints commemorated on March 29 include Bertold, Eustace of Luxeuil, Gwladys, Gwynllyw, and John Keble.

In *Eastern Orthodox Christianity*, it is the commemoration of martyrs Mark of Aresthusa, Cyril the Deacon of Heliopolis of Phoenicia, Saint John of Egypt, Saint Euscarhius the Confessor, Saints Jonah and Mark of the Pskov Caves, and the Repose of Elder Nicetas of the Roslavl Forests. (These are celebrated on April 11 by "Old Calendarists.)

Other Holidays (United States unless otherwise noted)

Some holidays are simply made up by individuals, companies, or other organizations, and whether they become widely adopted depends on whether people choose to celebrate them. Here are some opportunities to celebrate on March 29.

March 29 is America's Subway Day (Washington DC's Metrorail), The Festival of Smoke and Mirrors Day, National Mom and Pop Business Owners Day, Knights of Columbus Founders Day, Niagara Falls Runs Dry Day, Pickle Day, and Texas Love the Children Day.

The Resolute Conduct of the Earl of Warwick Previous to the Battle of Towton, Thomas Holloway after Henry Tresham

What Happened on March 29?

1461 – Battle of Towton

The Wars of the Roses were a series of wars fought between the House of Lancaster (whose symbol was a red rose) and the House of York (whose symbol was a white rose) for the throne of England. It lasted from 1455 to 1485, ending only when Henry VII, a Lancastrian, won the throne by defeating Richard III, then married Elizabeth of York to reunite the two houses and found the House of Tudor, which would rule for the next hundred years.

The Battle of Towton, which took place on March 29, 1461, was the single largest military engagement of the Wars of the Roses, in which 28,000 soldiers died out of the nearly 65,000 who fought for the two sides. It has been called "England's bloodiest battle," with more soldiers dying on English soil than in any other battle before or since. The battle was a decisive victory for the Yorkist forces, although the wars would continue to rage for another fourteen years.

The Battle of Towton is depicted in William Shakespeare's *Henry VI*, Part 3, Act 2, Scene 5.

1638 – First European Settlement in Delaware

The Swedes sent their first expedition to North America in late 1637, and on March 29, 1638, they sailed into Delaware Bay and landed near modern Wilmington, Delaware, at a site still known as Swedes' Landing. They built a fort at what became Wilmington, and their small colony, named New Sweden, grew to over 600 people.

In 1655, while Sweden was engaged in war with the Polish-Lithuanian Commonwealth, the Dutch, whose North American colonies occupied much of modern coastal New York and New Jersey, took advantage of the situation and sent an army to seize the Swedish colony for their own.

Dutch rule lasted until 1664, when the English conquered New Netherlands, beginning with the capture of New Amsterdam, which they renamed New York.

1806 – First US Federal Highway

On March 29, 1806, US President Thomas Jefferson signed the authorization to build the National Road (also called the Cumberland Road), a 620-mile long road that connected the Potomac and Ohio rivers and opened the American midwest for large numbers of settlers.

It was originally intended to stretch from Cumberland, Maryland, to St. Louis, Missouri, but funding ran out in 1837 and the road ended in Vandalia, Illnois.

Today, the modern US Route 40 travels much of the same route, and portions of the Cumberland—Baltimore road still use the name "National Pike." In 2002, the full road (finally extended to St. Louis) was designated "The Historic National Road, an All-American Road."

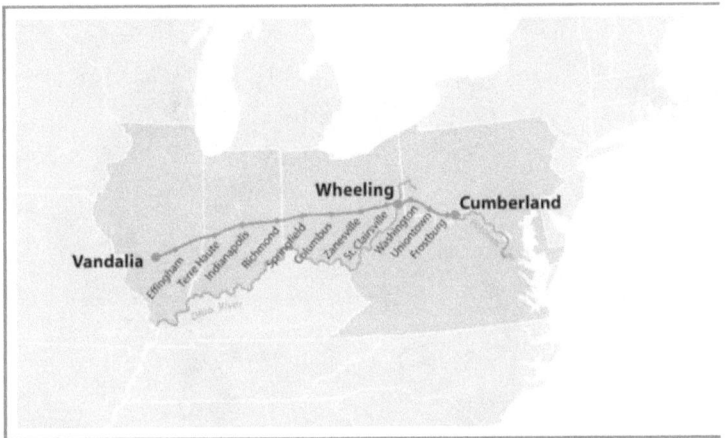

Route of the National Road

1882 – Knights of Columbus Chartered

The Knights of Columbus, the largest Catholic fraternal service organization in the world, was founded by Venerable Father Michael J. McGivney in New Haven, Connecticut, on March 29, 1882. Catholics were barred from many other fraternal organizations, such as Freemasonry, and the Knights of Columbus provided an alternative. It currently has over 1.8 million members in 15,000 councils and provides charitable services, offers mutual life insurance, and promotes Catholic education.

A Knights of Columbus World War I poster for the United War Work Campaign, 1918

1911 – The US Army Adopts the .45 Caliber M1911 Pistol

Beginning in the late 1890s, the US Army began searching for a self-loading (semi-automatic) pistol to replace an assortment of revolvers used by different units.

After extensive testing and trials of numerous weapons, the Colt .45 Caliber Automatic Pistol, Model 1911, designed by John Browning, was formally adopted as the standard US Army sidearm on March 29, 1911, and subsequently by the US Navy and Marine Corps in 1913.

With slight modifications, it continued to be the main US military sidearm from World War I through the Vietnam War, when the Beretta M9 was chosen as its replacement. However, the M1911 is still in widespread use by the Marine Corps and law enforcement in the United States.

Colt M1911 Automatic Pistol

1945 – End of the V-1 Attacks

The last V-1 "buzz bomb" rocket attack against England (and the last enemy action of any kind on British soil during World War II) occurred on March 29, 1945, in Datchworth, East Hertfordshire. The V-1 was a jet-powered early version of a cruise missile. Beginning on June 13, 1944, a week after D-Day, the Germans fired more than a hundred a day, over 9,500 in total. The attacks lasted until the final V-1 launch site on the French coast was overrun by advancing Allied troops.

A V-1 is rolled out by German Wehrmacht soldiers
(Bundesarchiv, Bild 146-1975-117-26 / Lysiak / CC-BY-SA)

1951 – Julius and Ethel Rosenberg are Convicted of Espionage

Julius Rosenberg, an electronics and nuclear engineer, along with his wife Ethel, were convicted of delivering information related to the atomic bomb to the Soviet Union on March 29, 1951, and sentenced to death. While there is some continuing controversy as to the amount and importance of the information Julius Rosenberg passed along, decoded Soviet cables confirmed that he was in fact a Soviet spy. The evidence of Ethel Rosenberg's active participation remains ambiguous.

1971 – William Calley is Convicted for the My Lai Massacre

US Army Lieutenant William Calley, Jr., was charged with premeditated murder for the deaths of 104 Vietnamese civilians near the village of My Lai on March 16, 1968. The My Lai Massacre, which took the lives of between 350 and 500 Vietnamese, created a global outcry when the story was revealed. Twenty-six soldiers were charged. On March 29, 1979, William Calley became the only person convicted. He was sentenced to life imprisonment, but ended up only serving three and a half years under house arrest.

1971 – Charles Manson is Sentenced to Death

Cult leader Charles Manson and his disciples were convicted of murdering Sharon Tate and others on January 25, 1971, and after sentencing hearings, was sentenced to death on March 29, 1971. The following year, the California Supreme Court abolished the death penalty in that state, which automatically changed the sentence to life imprisonment.

1974 – Mariner 10 Reaches Mercury

On March 29, 1974, the NASA space probe Mariner
10 reached its closest approach to the planet Mercury,
coming within 437 miles (703 kilometers) of that
world.

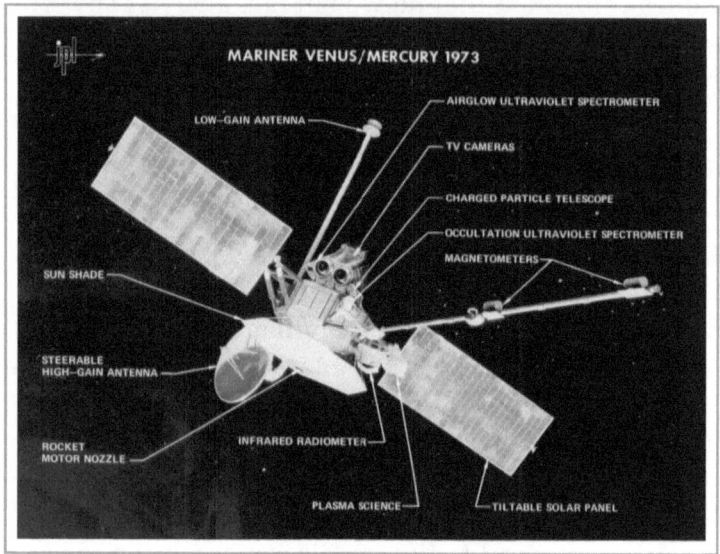

Mariner 10

1990 – The "Hyphen War" Begins

Following the Velvet Revolution in Czechoslovakia,
that country no longer wanted to be called the
Czechoslovak Socialist Republic (*Československá
socialistická republika*, or ČSSR), and planned to drop
"Socialist" from its name. Slovak politicians felt that
this made Slovakia less equal as part of the country,
and asked that the country's name be spelled with a
hyphen: Federation of Czecho-Slovakia (*Československá federatívna republika*) rather than
Czechoslovak Republic.

The initial compromise, passed into law on March 29, 1990, was to spell the name with a hyphen in Slovak and without a hyphen in Czech. This compromise was not sufficient. A month later, the country changed its name again to the Czech and Slovak Federative Republic (*Česká a Slovenská Federativní Republika* in Czech; *Federatívna* in Slovak), and in 1993, the Czech Republic and Slovakia became separate nations in what is known as the Velvet Divorce.

1999 – The Dow Breaks 10,000

On March 29, 1999, the Dow Jones Industrial Average, a popular stock market index, closed above 10,000 (10,006.78) for the first time in its history. It had broken 5,000 for the first time only four years previously. When it was first published in the mid-1880s, the Dow Jones Industrial Average began at 62.76, and hit a low of 41.22 following the stock market crash of 1929 that heralded the Great Depression.

Nazi era publicity photograph of aviatrix Hanna Reitsch following her award of the Iron Cross, the only woman in World War II to receive that distinction. (Credit: Bundesarchiv, Bild 183-B02092 / Schwahn / CC-BY-SA)

Who Was Born on March 29?

Art and Illustration

Mark Silvestri (March 29, 1958 –)

Comic book artist and publisher Mark Silvestri is known for his work on Marvel's Uncanny X-Men and Wolverine, and as one of the founders of Image Comics, which includes his own imprint, Top Cow.

Aviation and Space

William Oefelein (March 29, 1965 –)

Test pilot and NASA astronaut William Oefelein piloted the Space Shuttle Discovery for the STS-116 mission. He was dismissed from the astronaut corps for his affair with fellow astronaut Lisa Nowak, who became notorious when she was arrested while attempting to kidnap Oefelein's girlfriend (later wife) in 2007.

Hanna Reitsch (March 29, 1912 – August 24, 1979)

German aviatrix Hanna Reitsch is the only woman awarded the Iron Cross First Class during World War II. She established over 40 aviation records during her career, including becoming the first female helicopter pilot. A noted test pilot, she was involved in the development of the Focke-Achgelis Fa 61, the Messerschmitt Me 262 *Schwalbe* and the Me 163 *Komet*, and successfully landed the manned version of the V-1 flying bomb, known as the *Reichenberg*.

Enea Bossi (March 29, 1888 – 1963)

Italian-American aerospace engineer Enea Bossi is best known as the designer of the *Pedaliante,* the first airplane capable of human-powered flight. He also designed the first airplane built of stainless steel, the Budd BB-1 *Pioneer.*

Business

John M. Belk (March 29, 1920 – August 17, 2007

John Belk was head of the Belk department store chain and a four-term mayor of Charlotte, North Carolina.

Sam Walton (March 29, 1918 – April 5, 1992)

Sam Walton founded the retailers Walmart and Sam's Club, becoming the richest person in the United States according to Forbes magazine from 1982 to 1988.

Crime

Vincent "the Chin" Gigante (March 29, 1928 – December 19, 2005)

Former professional boxer Vincent Gigante worked his way up through the Luciano and Genovese crime families to become officially recognized as the most powerful crime boss in the United States. He feigned insanity in a long-running attempt to fool law enforcement, becoming known as "The Oddfather" and "The Enigma in the Bathrobe." He was convicted in 1997 and died in prison.

Vincent Gigante (Photo: Phil Stanziola)

Medicine

Karen Ann Quinlan (March 29, 1954 – June 11, 1985)

After lapsing into a persistent vegetative state, Karen Ann Quinlan was kept alive on a ventilator for several months. Her parents requested that the hospital discontinue active care and allow her to die naturally, resulting in a legal battle finally resolved in her parents' favor by the New Jersey Supreme Court. The case received national publicity and is considered an important part of the right-to-die controversy in the United States.

Music

Ондар Коӊгар-оол (Kongar-ol Ondar) (March 29, 1962 – July 25, 2013)

Kongar-ol Ondar was the international face of Tuvan throat singing, known as *хөөмей (khöömei)*.He appeared on American television programs including *The Late Show with David Letterman*, and was the subject of the 1999 documentary *Genghis Blues*. He appeared on two albums by Béla Fleck and the Flecktones, and released his own album, *Back Tuva Future*, on the Warner Brothers label.

Perry Farrell (March 29, 1959 –)

Singer-songwriter Perry Farrell was frontman for the group Jane's Addiction and created the touring festival Lollapalooza.

Patty Donahue (March 29, 1956 – December 9, 1996)

Patty Donahue was lead singer of the 1980s new wave group The Waitresses.

Terry Jacks (March 29, 1944 –)

Canadian singer-songwriter Terry Jacks is known for his 1973 hit song "Seasons in the Sun."

Vangelis (March 29, 1943 –)

Composer Ευάγγελος Παπαθανασίου (Evangelos Papathanassiou), professionally known as Vangelis, won an Academy Award for his score for the 1981 film *Chariots of Fire*.

Bob Haymes (March 29, 1923 – January 27, 1989)

Singer-songwriter and actor Bob Haymes is known for writing the classic song "That's All." He was the younger brother of singer and actor Dick Haymes.

E. Power Biggs (March 29, 1906 – March 10, 1977)

Organist E. Power Biggs is credited with sparking an American revival of traditional organ making. He received a star on the Hollywood Walk of Fame for his contributions to the recording industry.

Performing Arts

Lucy Lawless (March 29, 1968 –)

New Zealand actress Lucy Lawless is best known for playing the title character in the television series *Xena: Warrior Princess*.

Michel Hazanavicius (March 29, 1967 –)

Director, producer, and screenwriter Michel Hazanavicius won an Academy Award for Best Director for his Oscar-winning 2011 film *The Artist*.

Jill Goodacre (March 29, 1965 –)

Jill Goodacre is best known for her work as a Victoria's Secret lingerie model. She married singer-songwriter Harry Connick, Jr., in 1994.

Amy Sedaris (March 29, 1961 –)

Comedianne Amy Sedaris is best known for her role as Jerri Blank in the television series *Strangers with Candy*.

Annabella Sciorra (March 29, 1960 –)

Actress Annabella Sciorra had a leading role in the 1991 Spike Lee film *Jungle Fever*, starred in 1992's *The Hand that Rocks the Cradle*, and was nominated for an Emmy for her role as Gloria Trillo in the HBO television series *The Sopranos*.

Annabella Sciora (Photo: David Shankbone)

Christopher Lambert (March 29, 1957 –)

Christophe Lambert (known as Christopher outside the French-speaking world) is best known for playing the Highlander in the movie franchise of the same name and the role of Tarzan in the 1984 film *Greystoke.*

Marina Sirtis (March 29, 1955 –)

Marina Sirtis is best known for her role as Counselor Deanna Troi on the television series *Star Trek: The Next Generation* and its film spin-offs.

Brendan Gleeson (March 29, 1955 –)

English actor Brendan Gleeson won a 2009 Emmy for playing Winston Churchill in the film *Into the Storm,* but may be best known for his role as Hogwarts professor Mad-Eye Moody in the *Harry Potter* film series.

Dianne Kay (March 29, 1954 –)

Dianne Kay played Nancy Bradford on the television series *Eight is Enough.*

Bud Cort (March 29, 1948 –)

Bud Cort is best known for his roles in the cult classic films *Brewster McCloud* (1970) and *Harold and Maude* (1971).

Eric Idle (March 29, 1943 –)

Eric Idle is best known as a member of the English comedy group Monty Python.

Scott Wilson (March 29, 1942 –)

Scott Wilson received a Golden Globe nomination for his role in the 1980 film *The Ninth Configuration* (also known as *Twinkle, Twinkle, "Killer" Kane)* and had a leading role in the AMC series *The Walking Dead* from 2011 to 2013.

Terence Hill (March 29, 1939 –)

Italian actor Terence Hill is best known for his roles in "spaghetti westerns," most notably 1971's *Lo chiamavano Trinità (They Call Me Trinity)* and its 1972 sequel *Continuavano a chiamarlo Trinità (Trinity Is STILL My Name!).*

Eileen Heckart (March 29, 1919 – December 31, 2001)

Actress Eileen Heckart won an Academy Award as Best Supporting Actress for her role in the 1972 film *Butterflies are Free*, and was known for her roles on television series including *The Mary Tyler Moore Show* (two Emmy nominations) and daytime drama *One Life to Live*. At the age of 81, she appeared off-Broadway in the play *The Waverly Gallery*, receiving more awards for a single performance in a single season than any actress in theatre history. She is a member of the Theatre Hall of Fame.

Pearl Bailey (March 29, 1918 – August 17, 1990)

Actress and singer Pearl Bailey (see page 2) won a Tony for her role in the 1968 all-black production of *Hello, Dolly!*, and an Emmy for her role as a fairy godmother in an ABC Afterschool Special retelling of the Cinderella story. She had her own television series *(The Pearl Bailey Show)* in the 1970s and was appointed a Special Ambassador to the United Nations by US President Gerald Ford.

Phil Foster (March 29, 1913 – July 8, 1985)

Actor Phil Foster is best known for playing Frank, father of Laverne De Fazio, in the TV sitcom *Laverne & Shirley.*

Arthur O'Connell (March 29, 1908 – May 18, 1981)

Actor Arthur O'Connell received an Oscar nomination for his role in the 1956 film *Picnic*. Among his other well-known films are 1959's *Anatomy of a Murder*, the Elvis Presley films *Follow That Dream* and *Kissin' Cousins*, and the cult classic *The Seven Faces of Dr. Lao*.

Philip Ahn (March 29, 1905 – February 28, 1978)

Korean-American actor Pi Lip Ahn (안필립) was the first Asian-American ator to receive a star on the Hollywood Walk of Fame. He played a variety of Asian characters in films ranging from Shirley Temple's 1936 film *Stowaway* to Elvis Presley's 1966 *Paradise, Hawaiian Style*, but may be best known for playing Master Kan in the 1970s television series *Kung Fu*.

Philip Ahn

Warner Baxter (March 29, 1889 – May 7, 1951)

Warner Baxter began his career in silent films, and won the second-ever Academy Award for Best Actor for playing the Cisco Kid in 1929's *In Old Arizona*. He made over 100 films between 1914 and 1950.

Politics and News

John Major (March 29, 1943 –)

John Major was Prime Minister of the United Kingdom from 1990 to 1997.

Billy Carter (March 29, 1937 – September 25, 1988)

Younger brother of US President Jimmy Carter, Billy Carter was a popular press foil during his brother's presidency, and attempted to capitalize on his fame by promoting Billy Beer.

John McLaughlin (March 29, 1927 –)

Television personality and commentator John McLaughlin is known as the host and moderator of the TV debate program *The McLaughlin Group*.

Eugene McCarthy (March 29, 1916 – December 10, 2005)

Minnesota congressman and senator Eugene McCarthy was the first candidate to run against incumbent US President Lyndon B. Johnson for the 1968 Democratic nomination on an anti-Vietnam War platform.

Lavrentiy Beria (Лавре́нтий Бе́рия) (March 29, 1899 – December 23, 1953)

Soviet administrator Lavrentiy Beria was chief of the NKVD, the Soviet secret police, during the reign of Joseph Stalin, and later Deputy Premier of the Soviet Union following World War II. He administered the Gulag labor camps and organized the postwar Communist takeover of central and eastern European countries. He was deposed in a coup d'état organized by Nikita Khrushchev and shot in the basement of Moscow's Lubyanka (Лубя́нка) building, headquarters of the secret police he once commanded.

From left to right: Joseph Stalin (in background), Stalin's daughter Svetlana Alliluyeva (on lap), Lavrentiy Beria (with glasses), unknown man with headphones

John Tyler (March 29, 1790 – January 18, 1862)

John Tyler (facing page) was the tenth President of the United States and the first to become President without being elected to that office. He was elected Vice-President under William Henry "Tippecanoe" Harrison (hence the campaign slogan "Tippecanoe and Tyler, Too!").

When Harrison died after only a month in office, Tyler moved into the White House, took the oath of office, and proclaimed himself President rather than "Acting President," setting a precedent in American history. Called "His Accidency" for the way he became President, he broke with the Whig Party that elected him, and did not have enough political support to win election in his own right.

He became a member of the Confederate House of Representatives following the outbreak of the Civil War, becoming the first (and so far only) US President to serve in a foreign government following his time in office.

Religion

József Mindszenty (March 29, 1892 – May 6, 1975)

József Cardinal Mindszenty led the Roman Catholic Church in Hungary during World War II and under the postwar Communist government. After arrest and torture, he obtained political asylum in the US Embassy in Budapest, where he lived for fifteen years. He died in exile in Vienna, Austria.

Official White House portrait of President John Tyler by George
Peter Alexander Healy

Sports

Jennifer Capriati (March 29, 1976 –)

Tennis player Jennifer Capriata achieved the World #1 ranking in tennis in 2001, remaining in the top ten until 2004. She won a gold medal in the 1992 Barcelona Olympics.

Brian Jordan (March 29, 1967 –)

Athlete Brian Jordan played professional football for the Atlanta Falcons briefly, and professional baseball for the St. Louis Cardinals, Atlanta Braves, Los Angeles Dodgers, and Texas Rangers.

Billy Beane (March 29, 1962 –)

Baseball executive Billy Beane is known for applying statistical analysis (sabermetrics) to evaluate players for the Oakland Athletics, chronicled in the 2003 book *Moneyball*. He was played by Brad Pitt in the 2011 film of the same name.

Kurt Thomas (March 29, 1956 –)

American gymnast Kurt Thomas won a gold medal at the 1976 Summer Olympics. Two gymnastic moves, the Thomas Flair and the Thomas salto, were named for him, and in 2003 he was inducted into the International Gymnastics Hall of Fame.

Earl Campbell (March 29, 1955 –)

Nicknamed "The Tyler Rose," running back Earl Campbell is one of only three Heisman Trophy winners to have also been first NFL draft picks and elected to both the Pro Football Hall of Fame and the College Football Hall of Fame. He played for the Houston Oilers and the New Orleans Saints in his eight year professional career.

Walt Frazier (March 29, 1945 –)

Basketball point guard Walt Frazier led the New York Knicks to two NBA Championships and was inducted into the Naismith Memorial Basketball Hall of Fame in 1987.

Denny McLain (March 29, 1944 –)

Denny McLain pitched for the Detroit Tigers, Washington Senators, Oakland Athletics, and Atlanta Braves, becoming one of only 11 players in the 20th century to win 30 or more games in a single season. He was suspended for gambling activities, and following his baseball career, was convicted of embezzlement, mail fraud, and conspiracy, serving six years in prison.

Man o' War (March 29, 1917 – November 1, 1947)

Thoroughbred racehorse Man o' War (right, in his final race, 1920) was named the top US racehorse of the 20th century in polls conducted by *Blood-Horse Magazine, Sports Illustrated,* and the Associated Press. He and was elected to the US Racing Hall of Fame in 1957.

Don "Midnight" Miller (March 29, 1902 – July 28, 1979)

Football player and coach Don Miller was part of the famous "Four Horsemen" of the University of Notre Dame, called by head coach Knute Rockne "the greatest open field runner I ever had." He was named to the College Football Hall of Fame in 1970.

Cy Young (March 29, 1867 – November 4, 1955)

Major league baseball pitcher Cy Young achieved records for most career innings pitched, most career games started, most complete games, and others — several of which remain intact. Following his death, the Cy Young Award was created to honor the best pitcher of the previous baseball season.

Cy Young in 1908

Words and Literature

Elizabeth Hand (March 29, 1957 –)

Award-winning fantasy and thriller author Elizabeth Hand's best known works include the 1994 multiple award winners *Waking the Moon* and *Last Summer at Mars Hill*.

Christopher Lawford (March 29, 1955 –)

Son of actor Peter Lawford and socialite Pat Kennedy, Christopher Lawford was a nephew of US President John F. Kennedy who wrote the New York *Times* 2005 best-seller *Symptoms of Withdrawal* concerning his drug and alcohol addiction. He served as a Lecturer in Psychiatry at Harvard University, and as an executive with Universal Studios, where he acquired the film *American Graffiti*.

Judith Guest (March 29, 1936 –)

Author Judith Guest's first novel, *Ordinary People*, was made into a film that won the Academy Award for Best Picture. She is the great-niece of former US poet laureate Edgar Guest.

A Sunday Afternoon on the Island of La Grande Jatte, Georges
Seurat (detail)

Who Died on March 29?

Art

Georges Seurat (December 2, 1859 — March 29, 1891)

French post-impressionist painter Georges-Pierre Seurat is best known for developing the technique known as pointillism. His most famous work is *Un dimanche après-midi à l'Île de la Grande Jatte — 1884 (A Sunday Afternoon on the Island of La Grande Jatte — 1884)*, currently on display at the Art Institute of Chicago.

Business

John Jacob Astor (July 17, 1763 — March 29, 1848)

The first multi-millionaire in US history, John Jacob Astor (next page) built a large fur-trading empire that eventually spanned the continent. He sold Turkish opium to China, and later invested his fortune in New York City real estate and became a noted art patron.

Music

John Lewis (May 3, 1920 — March 29, 2001)

Pianist John Lewis was the musical director of the Modern Jazz Quartet.

John Jacob Astor, by Gilbert Stuart

The Singing Nun (October 17, 1933 — March 29, 1985)

Belgian singer-songwriter Jeanine Deckers entered the Dominican Order as Sister Luc Gabrielle. Under the name Sœur Sourire (Sister Smile), she recorded 1963's French language "Dominique," which became a worldwide hit. A 1965 movie, *The Singing Nun*, starring Debbie Reynolds, purported to chronicle her life, but Sister Gabrielle rejected it as "fiction."

She left the convent in 1966 because of conflicts with her superiors and with Catholic doctrine. She committed suicide, along with her partner of ten years, as a result of financial difficulties.

Mantovani (November 15, 1905 — March 29, 1980)

Annunzio Paolo Mantovani was an orchestra conductor who was Britain's most successful album act before the Beatles, playing light classical and popular music. His work was known for his signature "cascading strings" effect. He had 27 "Top 40" and 11 "Top Ten" albums in the US, and at one point had six albums in the Top Ten simultaneously.

Performing Arts

Paul Henreid (January 10, 1908 — March 29, 1992)

Actor Paul Henreid is best remembered for his role opposite Bette Davis in *Now, Voyager* and for playing Victor Laszlo in *Casablanca*.

Paul Henreid as Victor Laszlo from the trailer for *Casablanca*

Harry Ritz (May 22, 1907 — March 29, 1986)

Harry Ritz was a member of the comedy team The Ritz Brothers, who made numerous films between 1925 through the late 1960s.

The Ritz Brothers with trombonist Buddy Morrow. Harry Ritz is in the center. (Photo: William P. Gottlieb)

Politics, Law, and Government

Johnnie Cochran (October 2, 1937 — March 29, 2005)

Lawyer Johnnie Cochran is best known for leading the legal team that successfully defended O. J. Simpson against charges of having murdered his wife and another man.

Lee Atwater (February 27, 1951 — March 29, 1991)

Republican political consultant and strategist Lee Atwater advised US Presidents Ronald Reagan and George H. W. Bush, and chaired the Republican National Committee.

Luther Terry (September 15, 1911 — March 29, 1985)

US Surgeon General Luther Terry is best known for issuing a report concluding that cigarette smoking caused lung cancer and other illnesses.

Religion

Emanuel Swedenborg (January 29, 1688 — March 29, 1772)

Swedish scientist and philosopher Emanuel Swedenborg is best known for his Christian theological writing, which some believe to be divinely inspired. The "New Church" denominations (sometimes called Swedenborgians) form a religious movement based on Swedenborg's revelations.

Sports

Ted Kluszewski (September 10, 1924 — March 29, 1988)

Major League first baseman Ted Kluszewski (right) played for the Cincinnati Reds, the Pittsburgh Pirates, the Chicago White Sox, and the Los Angeles Angels in a career lasting from 1947 through 1961. He is a member of the Cincinnati Reds Hall of Fame and the National Polish-American Sports Hall of Fame.

März (March), by Hans Thoma

The Month of March

"Up from the sea, the wild north wind is blowing
Under the sky's gray arch;
Smiling I watch the shaken elm boughs, knowing
It is the wind of March."
— *"March," John Greenleaf Whittier*

In ancient Rome, March was the first month of the year. As the first month of spring, in the Mediterranean climate it marked the beginning of the military campaign season. That's why March (Martius) is named in honor of Mars, the Roman god of war.

Although the first month of the year was moved back to January sometime during the transition of Rome from a kingdom to a republic (historians differ), March was the first month of the year in Russia until the end of the 15th Century, and is the first month of the year in many other cultures and religions.

In the northern hemisphere, March 1 marks the beginning of meteorological spring. In the southern hemisphere, March is the equivalent of September, making southern hemisphere March the beginning of autumn.

March is one of the seven months that have 31 days in it. March starts on the same day of the week as November every year, and except for leap years starts on the same day as February. March starts on the same day of the week as the previous June except for leap years, and in leap years starts on the same day as the previous September and December.

March in Other Cultures

The month of March has different names in different languages. Some nations use calendars other than the Gregorian, and their months may overlap with November. Still, they often have a word for November itself.

Arabic (Egypt, Sudan, Yemen): مارس (Māris)

Chinese and Japanese: 三月

Croatian: Ožujak

Czech: Březen

Finnish: Maaliskuu (earthy month).

Greek: Μάρτιος

Hebrew: מרץ

Hindi: मार्च

Korean: 3 월에 (3 wol-e)

Old English: Hreþmōnaþ

Polish: Marzec

Russian: март

Slovene: Sušec

Ukrainian: березень (birch tree)

Vietnamese: 腩吧 (tháng ba)

March Superstitions

"Beware the Ides of March (March 15)!"

"March comes in like a lion and goes out like a lamb."

"April borrowed from March three days, and they were ill."

The first three days of March are unlucky "blind days." If rain falls on these days, farmers will have poor harvests.

Children born on Easter Day will be fortunate; children born on Good Friday are doomed to be unlucky.

"If Our Lord falls in Our Lady's lap/England will meet with a great mishap." (If Good Friday or Easter fall on Lady Day, March 25, the Feast of the Annunciation of Our Lady, national misfortune will befall.)

Clothes washed on Good Friday will never come clean.

Children should not climb trees on Good Friday.

Bread baked on Good Friday will never go moldy; eggs laid on Good Friday will no spoil.

Marriages that take place during Lent will have trouble.

"Married when March winds shrill and roar/Your home will be on a distant shore."

Good days to be married in March are March 3, 5, 13, 20, and 23. Which day? "Monday for wealth, Tuesday for health, Wednesday the best day of all, Thursday for losses, Friday for crosses, Saturday for no luck at all."

March Symbols

Birthstone Aquamarine and bloodstone, both representing courage.

Aquamarine

Birth Flowers Daffodils

Daffodil

March Events

Honorary Months

Presidents, Congresses, and nations around the world issue proclamations recognizing particular months to honor certain causes. These events generally fall in March. (All US unless otherwise noted.)

- American Red Cross Month
- Child Life Month
- Fire Prevention Month (The Philippines)
- Irish-American Heritage Month
- Colorectal Cancer Awareness Month
- National Caffeine Awareness Month
- National Celery Month
- National Cheerleading Safety Month
- National Flour Month
- National Frozen Food Month
- National Noodle Month
- National Nutrition Month
- National Peanut Month
- National Sauce Month
- Women's History Month (celebrated in Canada during October)

Women's Suffrage Demonstration 1917

"March Madness" (United States)

The NCAA Men's Division I Basketball Championship, popularly known as "March Madness" or the "Big Dance," is a single-elimination tournament to establish the champion college basketball team.

Moveable and Multi-Day Events

Some events take place over a specific week or time period. Start and finish dates may vary from year to year. Some events occur on different days each year (such as "fourth Saturday of a month").

Birkat Hachama (ברכת החמה) (Judaism)

According to the Talmud, the Sun was created at the vernal equinox position at the beginning of the

Jewish month of Nisan, established by tradition as March 25 on the Julian calendar.

The Birkat Hachama, "Blessing of the Sun" is recited when the vernal equinox occurs at sundown on a Tuesday, which happens every 28 years. When the Julian calendar gave way to the Gregorian calendar in 1582, the date shifted forward, and continues to shift slowly forward by approximately a day per century.

Birkat Hachama took place on April 8, 2009 (14 Nisan 5769), and will occur next on April 8, 2037 (23 Nisan 5797).

Birkat Hachama at the Western Wall, 2009

Earth Hour (International)

On Earth Hour, held on the last Saturday of March each year, households and business are urged to turn off all non-essential lights for one hour between 8:30pm to 9:30pm on each person's local time. The goal is to raise awareness of the need to take action on climate change.

Meat-Free Week (Australia)

Meat-Free Week, the last week in March, promotes vegetarianism.

National Cleaning Week (US)

National Cleaning Week, the last week of March, reminds us to start our spring cleaning.

Pediatric Nurse Practitioner Week (US)

Pediatric Nurse Practitioner Week is celebrated during the last week of March.

Seward's Day (Alaska)

Seward's Day, celebrated on the last Monday in March, commemorates the signing of the Alaska Purchase Treaty on March 30, 1867.

Easter Season

La crucifixion by El Greco

The Christian holiday of Easter in Western Christianity is held on the first Sunday after the Paschal Full Moon following the March equinox, which is officially set at March 21 by church reckoning. Easter itself can therefore occur as early as March 22 and as late as April 25, but occurs most often in April. In Eastern Christianity, which uses the Julian calendar, Easter occurs between April 4 and May 8. This also sets the date for the various events that lead up to Easter, most importantly the events of Holy Week.

Passion Sunday

The fifth Sunday of the Christian season of Lent is known as Passion Sunday in various Protestant denominations and by some traditionalist Catholics. Sometimes, the sixth Sunday of Lent is referred to as Passion Sunday, but it is more commonly known as Palm Sunday. Passion Sunday starts the two-week Passiontide, which ends on Holy Saturday, the day before Easter, commemorating the day that Jesus's body was laid in the tomb. The fifth Sunday of Lent can occur as early as March 8 (though the next time it will be that early is in 2285 CE), and as late as April 11.

Palm Sunday

The moveable feast of Palm Sunday commemorates the triumphant entry of Jesus into Jerusalem, an event mentioned in all four gospels. In many Christian churches, palm leaves are distributed to the worshippers. The earliest date for Palm Sunday is March 15, and the latest is April 18.

Maundy Thursday

The Thursday before Easter is Maundy Thursday, when the Last Supper took place. Because of its relation to Easter, the earliest day it can occur is March 19, and the latest it can occur is April 22.

Good Friday

Good Friday, observed during Holy Week on the Friday preceding Easter Sunday, commemorates the crucifixion of Jesus and his death at Calvary. Because of its relation to Easter, the earliest day it can occur is March 20, and the latest it can occur is April 23.

Holy Saturday

Sometimes called Easter Eve or Black Saturday, Holy Saturday commemorates the day in which Jesus's body lay in the tomb. Some mistakenly refer to this day as "Easter Saturday," but that properly describes the Saturday following Easter, the last day of Easter Week. The earliest it can occur is March 21, and the latest it can occur is April 24.

Easter

Easter celebrates the resurrection of Jesus Christ on the third day after his crucifixion. In the liturgical calendar, Easter follows the season of Lent, and begins the period known as Eastertide, which ends on Pentecost Sunday.

Easter is observed religiously in a morning service. In the U.S., it's also common to decorate Easter eggs and make Easter baskets of eggs and candy, often with the Easter bunny as a symbol. The White House traditionally hosts an egg hunt, and many communities have Easter parades.

Easter customs around the world include bonfires (Cyprus, western Sweden), men spanking women with a ceremonial whip (Czech Republic and Slovakia), egg fighting (Bulgaria), cross-country skiing and reading murder mysteries (Norway), and children dressed as witches collecting candy door-to-door (other Nordic countries).

Easter Eggs

Easter Monday

In some Roman Catholic and Eastern Orthodox cultures, the Monday after Easter is celebrated as a holiday. It is also known as Egg Nyte, featuring egg rolling competitions and dousing other people with water that had been blessed with holy water the previous day at mass. Easter Monday is also celebrated as Family Day in South Africa. In Guyana, people fly kites that were made on Holy Saturday. In Portugal, it is known as the Anjo (Ivy) Festival, in which people picnic in the countryside.

Śmigus-Dyngus (Poland, Hungary, Czech Republic, Slovakia)

The Monday after Easter in Poland and in the Polish diaspora is known as Śmigus-Dyngus, or simply Dyngus Day in the US. Boys throw water over girls they like and spank them with pussy willows. Girls avoid getting wet by giving boys "ransoms" of painted eggs.

Easter Week (Western Christianity), Bright Week (Eastern Christianity)

The period from Easter Sunday to the following Saturday is known as Easter Week. In both Western and Eastern Christianity (where it's known as Bright Week), the resurrection continues to be celebrated in church services. Easter Tuesday is a public holiday in the Australian state of Tasmania.

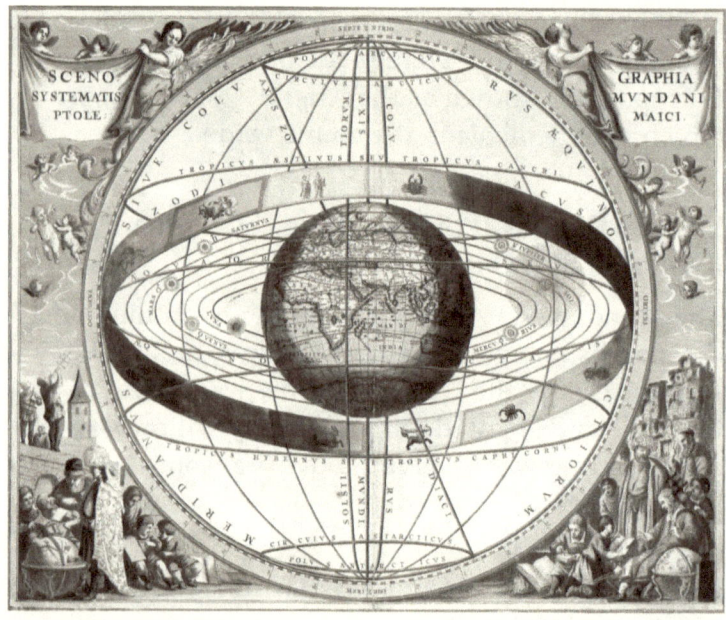

Scenography of the Ptolemaic Cosmography, by Johannes van Loon, based on Andreas Cellarius's *Harmonia Macrocosmica,* 1660

March Zodiac Signs

From the perspective of someone on Earth, the Sun appears to move through the sky throughout the year, along a path astronomers call the *ecliptic plane*. The ecliptic plane is divided into twelve constellations, known as the zodiac, based on traditionally observed patterns of stars. On your birthday, you can't see your constellation, because it's in the daytime sky.

The zodiac was first developed by Babylonian astronomers about 2,500 years ago. Because they were unaware that the Earth wobbles like a spinning top (known as *precession*), they didn't make allowance for the fact that the Sun's path through the zodiac changes over time.

That means there are now two sets of dates for your birth sign. The *tropical dates* are the original Babylonian dates; the *sidereal dates* tell you where the Sun actually appears as it moves along its annual path.

For March 29, the tropical sign is **Aries**, and the sidereal sign is **Pisces.**

Pisces

Tropical February 20 to March 20
Sidereal March 15 to April 14

In the Roman legend of Venus and her son Cupid, they escaped the clutches of Typhon, known as the "father of all monsters," by transforming into fish and tying themselves together with rope. That's why the name Pisces is plural for fish. The constellation appears as a somewhat ragged "V" shape, representing the rope, with the "fish" located at the two rope ends.

In astrology, Pisces is a water sign, compatible with the other water signs Cancer and Scorpio, as well as with the earth signs Taurus, Virgo, and Capricorn. Pisceans are supposed to be imaginative, compassionate, unworldly, secretive, and escapist.

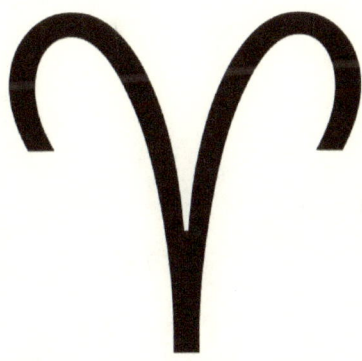

Aries

Tropical March 21 to April 19
Sidereal April 15 to May 15

In Greek mythology, Aries is a ram with golden wings and golden wool who rescued the twins Phrixus and Helle from certain death. Although Helle died in the rescue attempt, the grateful Phrixus sacrificed the ram to Zeus. The golden fleece from the sacrificed ram played a prominent part in the later myth of Jason and the Argonauts.

In astrology, Aries, a fire sign, is compatible with the other fire signs of Gemini, Leo, and Sagittarius, and to a lesser extent with air signs Scorpio and Libra. Arians are supposed to be adventurous, enthusiastic, quick-tempered, and impulsive.

Illustration by Edward Penfield

What Day of the Week is March 29?

On what day of the week does March 29 fall?

Surprisingly, this isn't an easy question. Because the calendar year is 365 days long (366 in leap years), it doesn't divide evenly by the seven days of the week.

Also, the Earth goes around the Sun in about 365-1/4 days, so a calendar tends to drift over time. That's why the same date falls on different weekdays in different years.

This is made even more complicated by a change in calendars that took place in 1582. Our modern calendar has its roots in ancient Rome, in a calendar reform conducted by Julius Caesar. Caesar commissioned mathematicians to attack the problem, and they came up with the idea of leap years, and thus standardized the calendar for centuries to come. This was called the Julian calendar.

Over time, however, the small errors in Caesar's calculation compounded. That's why Pope Gregory XIII commissioned the Gregorian calendar, used in most of the world today. Some countries converted in 1582, when the calendar was first developed; some converted later; other still haven't changed.

Gregorian and Julian aren't the only types of calendars. The Hebrew year, the Islamic year, and many other calendars are used in different parts of the world and among different people.

You can convert Gregorian dates to other calendars, including the Hebrew calendar, the Islamic calendar, and even the Mayan calendar by visiting the Fourmilab Calendar Converter at http://www.fourmilab.ch/documents/calendar/.

Chinese calendar systems are quite complex and have changed several times; a full discussion is far beyond the scope of this book. If you're interested, you can find information here: http://www.hermetic.ch/cal_stud/chinese_cal.htm.

On Names and Dates

Historians use "CE" (Common Era) and "BCE" (Before the Common Era) instead of the more common "AD" (Anno Domini, or Year of Our Lord) and "BC" (Before Christ), reflecting the fact that the year-numbering system established by the Gregorian calendar is used throughout the world in many countries not culturally Christian.

The CE/BCE designation dates back to at least 1708, and has been adopted as a standard by the United Nations and the Universal Postal Union. Because this series of books covers events and people of all nations and cultures, we use the CE/BCE terms.

The abbreviation "O.S." ("Old Style") on some dates refers to the fact that the Russian Empire did not switch from the Julian to the Gregorian calendar at the same time as the rest of Europe, and therefore some figures and events have two dates.

Also, in the Julian calendar in England in the 16th century, the year began on March 25 rather than January 1. To avoid confusion with Gregorian dates, dates between January and March were often written using both years.

People and events whose original names are not in the Western alphabet have their native names (where possible) in the appropriate script shown in parenthesis. If you are using an e-reader to access an electronic version of this book, all characters don't always display on all devices.

A 50-year brass perpetual calendar.

Cartoon by John T. McCutcheon

Copyright, Credit, and Contact

Follow Us

Our blog Dobson's Improbable History (http://
improbhistory.blogspot.com) features short articles on events
and people associated with each day, and updates several
times each week. You can also get a daily "What Happened
In History" message and all the latest Timespinner Press
news by following us on Facebook at https://
www.facebook.com/TimespinnerPress. Our Twitter feed
@SidewiseThinker links you to all our News of the Day.

Contact Us

Find an error or a format problem? Want information about
the series, about us, or about when the volume for your
special day might be available? Please email us at
editor@timespinnerpress.com. (We also take requests if your
special day isn't yet complete. Please give us at least six
weeks' notice if possible.)

Editorial Note

Every once in a while, I have a personal connection to the
date at hand. My great-great-great-great-great grandfather
was Judge John Tyler Sr., college roommate of Thomas
Jefferson and governor of Virginia, and father of the 10th
President of the United States, John Tyler, born March 29,
1790, making Tyler my great-great-great-great uncle.

Sources

We owe a great debt to Wikipedia, which is our first stop for research. We attempt to make independent confirmation of all important dates and facts through a variety of other sources. Other sources we frequently use include the Library of Congress; "on this day" listings from Encyclopedia Britannica, the New York Times, and the BBC; and, of course, the always essential Google.

All art and photographs are either in the public domain, used under a Creative Commons license, or with a "fair use" justification, and most frequently come from Wikimedia Commons and the Library of Congress Prints and Photographs Division.

Attribution is provided where possible, or as requested by the copyright owner, or when there is particular historical significance, listed below. For information about any particular illustration or photograph, please contact us.

Credits

- The cover photograph of soldiers from the Terracotta Army in China was taken in 2008 by "High Contrast," and is used here under CC-BY-SA 3.0 Germany.

- The illustration of the month of March on the back cover and the frontispiece is from the French Gothic illuminated manuscript *Les Très Riches Heures du duc de Berry* by the Limbourg Brothers, Jean Colombe, and an intermediate painter whose name is lost to history. It is in the public domain because its copyright has expired.

- The photograph of the excavation site for the Terracotta Army was taken in 2008 by Gustavo Madico. It is used here under CC-BY-SA 2.0.

- The 1968 publicity photograph of Pearl Bailey appearing on *The Ed Sullivan Show* is in the public domain because it was published in the United States between 1923 and 1977 without a copyright notice.

Photographs Division. It was deeded to the public domain by the donor as part of the Instrument of Gift.

- The 2008 photograph of Annabella Sciorra was taken by David Shankbone and is used here under CC-BY-SA 3.0.

- The 1968 publicity photograph of Philip Ahn as Master Kan from the *Kung Fu* television series is in the public domain because it was published in the United States between 1923 and 1977 without a copyright notice.

- The photograph of Lavrentiy Beria with Joseph Stalin's family is in the public domain according to Article 6 of Law No. 231-FZ of the Russian Federation.

- The official White House portrait of US President John Tyler was painted in 1859 by George Peter Alexander Healy. It is in the public domain because its copyright has expired.

- The 1920 photograph of Man o' War is in the public domain because its copyright has expired.

- The 1908 photograph of Cy Young pitching is from the George Grantham Bain Collection at the US Library of Congress's Prints and Photographs Division. It is in the public domain because its copyright has expired.

- Georges Seurat's 1880s painting *A Sunday Afternoon on the Island of La Grande Jatte* is in the public domain because its copyright has expired. The painting itself is in the collection of the Art Institute of Chicago.

- The 1794 painting of John Jacob Astor by Gilbert Stuart is in the public domain because its copyright has expired.

- The screenshot of Paul Henreid from the trailer for the 1942 film *Casablanca* is in the public domain because it was published in the United States between 1923 and 1977 without a copyright notice.

- The 1947 photograph of the Ritz Brothers with trombonist Buddy Morrow was taken by William P. Gottlieb, and is part of a collection of jazz photographs now in the Library of Congress Music Division. As of 2010, the photograph is in the public domain in accordance with the wishes of William Gottlieb.

- The pre-1818 painting of Emanuel Swedenborg is by Carl Frederik von Breda. It is in the public domain because its copyright has expired.

- The photograph of Ted Kluszewski first appeared in the November 1954 issue of *Baseball Digest*. It is in the public domain because, although it was originally copyrighted, the copyright was not renewed.

- The painting *März (March)* is from the calendar book *Festkalender* by Hans Thoma. It is in the pubic domain because its copyright has expired.

- The photograph of aquamarine has been released into the public domain.

- The photograph of daffodils is by "Myrabella," and is licensed under CC-BY-SA 3.0.

- The 1917 Women's Suffrage demonstration comes from the Library of Congress, Prints and Photographs Division, LC-USZ62-31799 DLC, and is in the public domain because its copyright has expired.

- The 2009 photograph of Birkat Hachama at the Western Wall is by "Ingo," and is used here under CC-BY-SA 3.0.

- The painting *La Crucifixión* by El Greco is located in the Museo del Prado. It is in the public domain because its copyright has expired.

- The photograph of Czechoslovakian Easter eggs was taken by Jan Kameníček, who has released the image into the public domain.

- The zodiac chart was created around 1660 by Johannes van Loon, based on work by Andreas Cellarius, for the book *Harmonia Macrocosmica*. It is in the public domain because its copyright has expired.

- The 1906 automobile calendar is by Edward Penfield, and is in the collection of the Library of Congress Prints and Photographs Division. It is in the public domain because its copyright has expired.

- The 50-year perpetual calendar photograph is in the public domain.

- The cartoon by John T. McCutcheon is from his 1905 collection *The Mysterious Stranger and Other Cartoons by John T. McCutcheon*. It is in the public domain because its copyright has expired.

License Description and Terms

Aside from material purely in the public domain, photographs and other material in this book are used under specific licenses permitting free use, usually with an attribution requirement. For full text and terms of these licenses, click or enter the appropriate links below. If you believe there is an error in the copyright status or attribution of any of these images, please email us.

- Creative Commons Attribution 2.0 Generic (CC-BY 2.0): http://creativecommons.org/licenses/by/2.0/deed.en
- Creative Commons Attribution-Share Alike 3.0 Generic (CC-BY-SA 3.0): http://creativecommons.org/licenses/by-sa/3.0/
- Creative Commons Attribution-Share Alike 2.5 Generic (CC-BY-SA 2.5): http://creativecommons.org/licenses/by-sa/2.5/deed.en
- Creative Commons Attribution-Share Alike 2.0 Generic (CC-BY-SA 2.0): http://creativecommons.org/licenses/by/2.0/deed.en
- Creative Commons Attribution-Share Alike 1.0 Generic (CC-BY-SA 1.0): http://creativecommons.org/licenses/by-sa/1.0/deed.en
- CC0 1.0 Universal (CC0 1.0) Public Domain Dedication (CC0 1.0) http://creativecommons.org/publicdomain/zero/1.0/deed.en
- GNU Free Documentation License (GFDL): http://en.wikipedia.org/wiki/Wikipedia:Text_of_the_GNU_Free_Documentation_License

Timespinner
Press